The Amazing Universe

Paul Shipton

Level 4
Series Editor: Melanie Williams

Pearson Education Limited
Edinburgh Gate, Harlow
Essex CM20 2JE, England
and Associated Companies throughout the world.

ISBN 0582 465753

First published by
Penguin Books 2002

1 3 5 7 9 10 8 6 4 2

Text copyright © 2002 Paul Shipton
Illustrations copyright © 2002 Nick Hawken, pages 4-5, 28-29

Acknowledgements
Photos and artwork are reproduced by courtesy of
DK Picture Library, pages 9, 10, 13, 16, 18, 20, 26;
Galaxy Picture Library, pages 21, 24, 27;
The Kobal Collection, pages 8 (Paramount), 14 (Universal), 15 (Warner Bros – center, Columbia);
The Mary Evans Picture Library, pages 14, 15;
Science Photo Library, pages 6, 7, 10, 11, 12, 13, 17, 18-19, 19, 22, 23, 27

The moral right of the author has been asserted

Design by Wendi Watson
Colour reproduction by Spectrum Colour Ltd. Ipswich
Printed in Great Britain by Scotprint, Haddington

Published by Pearson Education Limited in association with Penguin Books Ltd,
both companies being subsidiaries of Pearson Plc

For a complete list of the titles available in the Penguin Young Readers series
please write to your local Pearson Education office or to:
Marketing Department, Penguin Longman Publishing,
80 Strand London WC2R 0RL

Contents

Our Solar System

Our solar system is nothing more than a tiny, tiny part of the whole universe. There are nine planets and the sun, which is a star. The sun is not a very big star compared to others in the universe, but it is still huge. All nine planets go around the sun. The time it takes for each of the planets to orbit the sun is very different.

Pluto's orbit takes 247.68 Earth years!

Pluto

Neptune

Uranus

Saturn

The sun is a giant ball of burning gas with a temperature in the middle of 15 million degrees centigrade. It is over 5 billion years old.

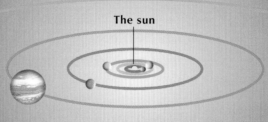

The sun

Mercury's orbit takes only 87.97 Earth days.

The nine planets spin too as they orbit. One spin of the Earth takes 24 hours – one day.

Jupiter

Mars   Earth   Venus   Mercury

WOW!

A Venus "day" (243 Earth days) is longer than a Venus "year" (225 Earth days)!

The Speed of Light

The light from the sun takes just over eight minutes to get to Earth. With Earth 145.6 million kilometers from the sun, that means the light travels at 294,400 kilometers in one second. That's very fast!

Scientists think that nothing else can travel as fast as the speed of light.

WOW!
A car traveling at 96 kilometers an hour would take 177 years to go from the sun to the Earth!

Scientists use "light-years" to talk about the enormous distances between stars. A "light-year" is the distance light travels in one year. That distance is 9.6 trillion kilometers!

Proxima Centauri is the nearest star to our sun. Our sun's light takes 4.2 years to get there, so we say this star is 4.2 light-years away from our sun. This also means that the light is four years old when it gets there!

Transportation

On TV and in the movies, humans and aliens travel from star to star in huge spacecraft. The spacecraft travel huge distances, and can go faster than the speed of light.

The Starship Enterprise in Star Trek goes faster than light.

In the *Star Wars* movies, there are all kinds of spacecraft. Here is the Millennium Falcon. It fights in space like an airplane.

Will we ever see real spaceships like those in movies?

Mercury

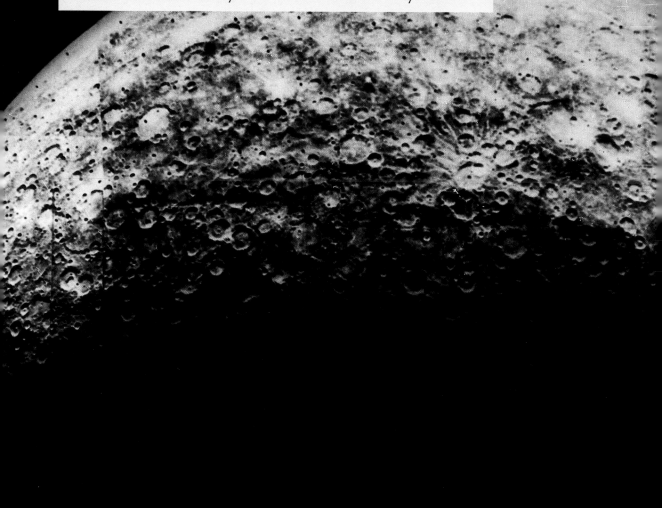

Mercury is the nearest planet to the sun. It spins slowly, one spin taking 58.6 Earth days. But it has the quickest orbit around the sun of 88 Earth days. It is 912 million kilometers away from Earth. That's close!

When Mercury faces the sun, it is very hot – 426 degrees centigrade. But the part of Mercury that is turned away from the sun is very cold.

The surface of Mercury looks like our moon.

Venus

Venus has been called "Earth's sister." This was because scientists used to think there might be living things on Venus as it is covered by clouds. They know now that Venus's yellow clouds are poisonous and the planet's surface is hotter than Mercury's. So Venus has a new name: "Earth's ugly sister!"

WOW!

Venus looks so bright that people used to think that it was a star. Here Venus shines above the moon.

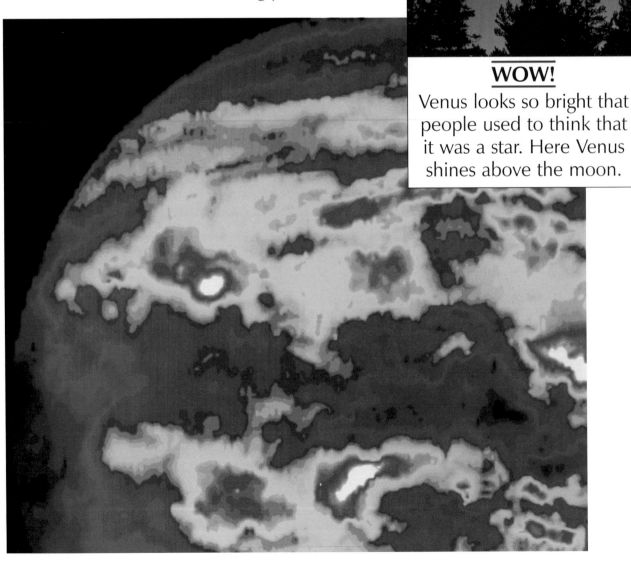

Earth

Earth is the third nearest planet to the sun.

Our planet has a perfect balance of atmosphere, temperature, water, and weather patterns. This balance means that there are thousands and thousands of different plants and animals on our planet – more than we can count! That makes Earth the most amazing planet of all! The atmosphere around the Earth stops us getting too hot or cold.

WOW!
In 1875, three men tried to go as high as they could into the atmosphere. After nine kilometers, two died.

Earth's Moon

We have one moon that orbits the planet Earth. This orbit takes 27.3 days. The moon is like a mirror for the sun's light and is often the brightest thing in the night sky. But it has no light of its own.

The moon spins around at the same time as it goes round the Earth. This means we only ever see one side of the moon!

The moon over Vancouver, Canada

Mars

Mars is called "The Red Planet" because of its color in the night sky.

Most of Mars's surface is a desert, and terrible wind storms cover the planet. It is cold, too – a warm day on Mars is a little like a day at Earth's Antarctic! Living things need water and there is no water on Mars now. But there is ice, which means there was once water on Mars.

Pictures of Mars

Aliens

People have always been interested in Mars.
In H. G. Wells's famous book *The War of the Worlds*,
written in 1898, aliens from Mars attack Earth. This book
was the first of many about Martians visiting Earth.

Not all aliens come from Mars. In the movie *ET*, ET is an
alien from the Green Planet, who comes to Earth in a
spacecraft. He makes friends with some children who
help him get back home to his planet.

Writers of movies, TV shows, and books imagine aliens in different ways. Some aliens look like we do! Others look different, but they still look friendly, just like ET.

Some aliens travel in huge machines. This picture and the one on page 14 come from the book The War of the Worlds.

This picture is from the movie Men in Black. *The cop has found an alien.*

An alien from Mars Attacks

But are there real aliens somewhere in the universe?

Some people believe that aliens have already visited our planet. A few people even say that they have seen aliens and have been taken to alien spacecraft. What do you think? As you read this book, maybe an alien on a planet in another galaxy is looking at the stars. Maybe it is imagining what aliens are like. Maybe it is thinking about YOU!

Jupiter, Saturn, Uranus, and Neptune

They are all huge planets. Jupiter is the biggest. More than 1,300 Earths could fit inside Jupiter, which is mostly gas. Jupiter, Saturn, Uranus, and Neptune all have rings. Jupiter's rings are made of dust. Saturn's and Neptune's are made of ice and rock.

WOW!
Uranus's rings go from top to bottom. Maybe something hit the planet a long time ago and knocked it on its side.

Saturn's rings are different from any others. They stretch across a distance of 588,060 kilometers, 21 times the width of the Earth, twice as wide as Jupiter itself!

Jupiter is the biggest planet and it has 16 moons. Saturn is the second biggest. It has moons, too. The biggest is called Titan.

Jupiter with two moons

WOW!
Saturn is so light that it would float if you could put it in water. But you would need a *lot* of water!

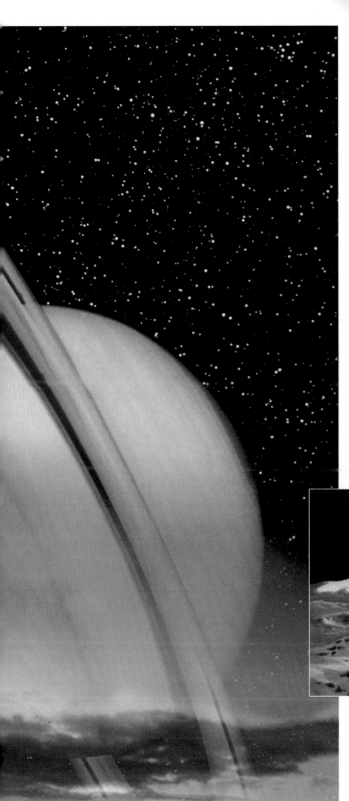

Pluto

Pluto, the smallest planet, is also the farthest from the sun . . . most of the time. For 20 years of its 248-year orbit, it is closer to the sun than Neptune is.

No spacecraft has visited Pluto. Scientists cannot be sure about its appearance.

One of Neptune's moons, Triton, is bigger than the planet Pluto! Was Triton once a planet that was pulled into Neptune's orbit?

Neptune seen from Triton

WOW!
Pluto was not discovered until 1930!

Asteroids

Giant rocks in space, called asteroids, also orbit the sun. Most are in the Asteroid Belt, a ring between Mars and Jupiter. About once every million years, an asteroid is pulled out of its orbit and hits our planet. In the past, these have been small asteroids but if a big asteroid hit Earth, it could kill everything.

WOW!
An asteroid hit Earth about 65 million years ago. Did it kill the dinosaurs?

Comets

Comets also orbit the sun. They are made of ice and rock. When their orbit takes them near the sun, we can see their long tails of ice and dust.

Once people thought comets were a sign of disaster. In 1066 there was a comet in the sky. Prince William attacked England that year and King Harold died.

This is Halley's Comet, which can be seen from Earth every 76 years. It will be back in 2062.

Galaxies

Our sun is just one of 200 billion stars in a galaxy called the Milky Way. Galaxies are huge groups of stars, gas, and dust. If you wanted to count every star in our galaxy, it would take you over 6,000 years!

Like all galaxies, the Milky Way is spinning. Our sun is 25,000 light-years away from the middle of our galaxy. It is on one of the galaxy's long arms.

The Milky Way is just one of hundreds of billions of galaxies. We see some of these galaxies in the night sky. Sometimes you can see the galaxy Andromeda.

Andromeda

The Milky Way

WOW!

Andromeda is the farthest thing anyone has ever seen without a telescope. It is 2.5 million light-years away. When we see this galaxy, the light we see is over 2 million years old. It began its journey before there were humans on Earth!

Like everything in space, galaxies are moving. Some galaxies orbit bigger galaxies. Sometimes whole galaxies crash into each other. When this happens, thousands of new stars are made.

Here are two galaxies. They are sharing stars because they are so close together.

WOW!

One day our galaxy might crash into our neighbor, Andromeda. But don't worry. This won't happen for 5 billion years.

New Stars

The universe is always changing. Every day new stars are born. Most new stars are made in groups inside giant clouds of gas. As the gas comes together, it gets hotter. Finally, new stars are made.

This amazing picture from the Hubble Space Telescope shows a group of stars called the Pleiades, or Seven Sisters. These stars were born 50 million years ago – that makes them young stars. They are 410 light-years away.

The Hubble Space Telescope

Telescopes let us see many more stars and galaxies. One of the most famous is the Hubble Space Telescope. Since 1990, it has orbited Earth in space, sending us amazing pictures of far-away stars and galaxies. Some of these pictures are of galaxies never seen before! The pictures are so good because the telescope is outside Earth's atmosphere.

WOW!

Astronauts have to walk in space to fix the Hubble telescope. Here a woman astronaut practices under water.

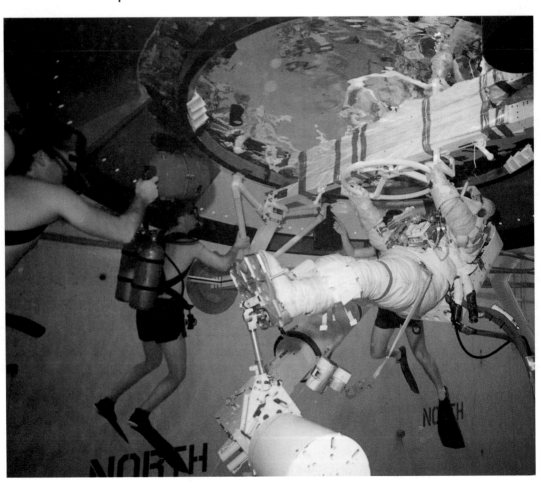

Supernovas

Stars die, too. When small stars die, they turn red and grow enormous. Big stars die in a huge explosion called a supernova. In our galaxy, there are only two or three supernovas every hundred years.
For a few months, the light of a supernova can be brighter than a whole galaxy.

WOW!

In 1054, a supernova was seen over China. After 900 years, scientists discovered the clouds of gas left after that supernova.

Black Holes

When the biggest supernovas finally die, they can turn into one of the strangest things in the universe – a black hole. The pull from inside a black hole is so strong that not even light can get out.

There is a black hole at the middle of our galaxy, the Milky Way.

WOW!

Do black holes change time? If you went into a black hole, would you come out in a different time?

You are here!

The Milky Way

Black hole

The Birth of the Universe

All these hundreds of billions of galaxies together make what we call the universe.

Most scientists think that the universe began about 13 billion years ago. In its first second, the universe grew from a tiny object to a universe 20,000 light-years across. It grew so quickly that scientists call that time the Big Bang.

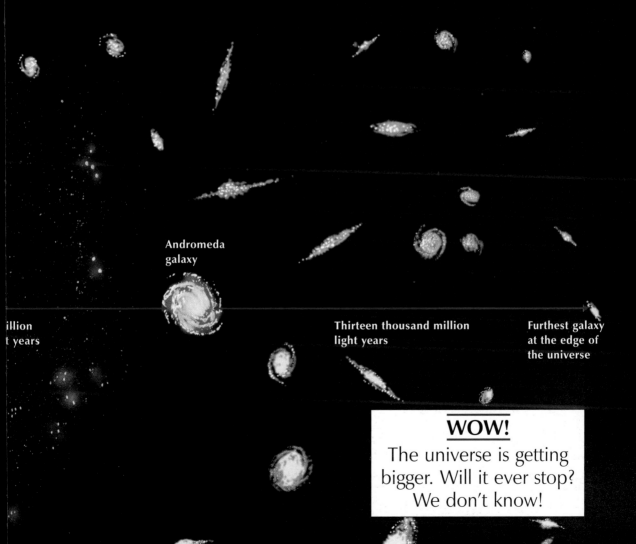

Andromeda galaxy

illion
t years

Thirteen thousand million
light years

Furthest galaxy
at the edge of
the universe

WOW!
The universe is getting bigger. Will it ever stop? We don't know!

Glossary

asteroid	a giant rock in space
atmosphere	a mixture of gases around the Earth
billion, US (*in this book*)	1,000,000,000
comet	you can see its long tail from Earth
degrees centigrade	15 million degrees centigrade = 27 million degrees Fahrenheit (page 5)
galaxy	a huge group of stars, gas, and dust
kilometer	8 kilometers = 5 miles
orbit	the Earth orbits (goes round) the Sun
spacecraft	people travel into space in these
supernova	the huge explosion when a big star dies
telescope	you can see the stars through this
universe	all the hundreds of billions of galaxies together

Activities

Before You Read

1. The Earth is one of nine planets in the solar system. How many of the other eight can you name?

Look at page 4 to check your answers!

After You Read

2. Look through the book and write the names of the planets in the sentences.

a. _____ is the nearest to the sun.

b. _____ has poisonous yellow clouds.

c. The moon orbits _____.

d. _____ is sometimes called "The Red Planet."

e. _____ is the biggest planet.

f. _____ is famous for its rings.

g. The rings around _____ go from top to bottom.

h. _____ has a moon, Triton, that is bigger than Pluto.

i. _____ was discovered in 1930.

Activities

3. How much do you know about the universe? Find the answers to these questions.

   a. What is the smallest planet in our solar system?

   b. Has an asteroid ever hit Earth?

   c. How long does light take to travel from the sun to Earth?

   d. What is the name of our galaxy?

   e. How far away is the nearest star?

   f. How old is the universe?

   g. What object in space might change time?

   h. What happens just before a star dies?

4. Imagine you meet an alien! What do you think it will look like?

Draw a picture of an alien and then write a short description of your alien and its planet.